Chicken Cacciatore Recipes

A Delicious Journey Through Classic and Creative Chicken Cacciatore Dishes

CHICKEN CACCIATORE RECIPES

First edition. December 8, 2023.

ISBN: 979-8223468608

Written by Sammy Andrews.

Table of Contents

Sammy Andrews

Chapter 1: Introduction to Chicken Cacciatore

The Allure of Chicken Cacciatore

Chicken Cacciatore, or "Pollo alla Cacciatora" in Italian, is a rustic and heartwarming dish that has captured the hearts and taste buds of food lovers around the world. Its origins can be traced back to the rustic kitchens of Italy, where it was traditionally prepared by hunters (hence the name "cacciatore," which means "hunter" in Italian) after a successful hunt.

The essence of Chicken Cacciatore lies in its simplicity and the use of fresh, wholesome ingredients. It's a dish that celebrates the flavors of the Italian countryside, combining tender chicken with aromatic herbs, tomatoes, bell peppers, onions, and sometimes even wine or olives. The result is a savory, soul-satisfying meal that brings people together at the dinner table.

A Brief History

The history of Chicken Cacciatore is as rich and varied as its flavors. While it's firmly rooted in Italian culinary tradition, it has evolved over the years to include a wide range of interpretations. Originally, hunters would prepare the dish with whatever ingredients were readily available in the countryside, making it a versatile and adaptable recipe from the start.

In Italy, regional variations of Chicken Cacciatore exist. For instance, in southern Italy, olives and capers are often added to the dish, giving it a distinct Mediterranean flavor. In the north, mushrooms might find their way into the recipe, creating a unique and earthy twist.

Essential Ingredients

To embark on your own Chicken Cacciatore journey, you'll need a handful of essential ingredients:

Chicken: Traditionally, chicken thighs or drumsticks are used, but you can also use bone-in, skin-on chicken breasts or a whole chicken cut into pieces.

Tomatoes: Fresh or canned, tomatoes form the base of the sauce. Some recipes call for tomato paste or puree as well.

Aromatics: Onions, garlic, and bell peppers add depth and flavor to the dish.

Herbs: Fresh basil, oregano, and thyme are often used, though dried herbs work beautifully too.

Wine (Optional): Red or white wine can be added for complexity and depth of flavor.

Olives or Capers (Optional): For a Mediterranean touch, consider adding green or black olives or capers.

Mushrooms (Optional): If you enjoy mushrooms, they can be a delightful addition.

Olive Oil: High-quality extra virgin olive oil is a must for sautéing and enhancing the dish's richness.

Cooking Techniques

Chicken Cacciatore is known for its slow-simmered, savory goodness. Here are a few key cooking techniques to master:

Sautéing: The initial step involves browning the chicken and aromatics in a hot pan. This adds a layer of flavor to the dish.

Simmering: After the initial sauté, the chicken and ingredients are simmered in the tomato-based sauce until the chicken is tender and the flavors meld together.

Seasoning: Don't forget to season your dish with salt and pepper to taste, and adjust the herbs and spices to suit your preference.

As you progress through this cookbook, you'll learn not only the classic preparation of Chicken Cacciatore but also creative variations and modern twists on this beloved Italian dish. Whether you're a seasoned home cook or a novice in the kitchen, you'll find something here to delight your taste buds and elevate your culinary skills.

Chapter 2: Traditional Italian Chicken Cacciatore

The Classic Recipe with a Step-by-Step Guide

When it comes to Chicken Cacciatore, the traditional Italian recipe is the gold standard. This timeless dish encapsulates the rustic flavors of Italy, making it a favorite in households around the world. In this chapter, we'll take you through the steps of creating an authentic Italian Chicken Cacciatore that will transport your taste buds to the rolling hills of Tuscany.

Ingredients:

- 4 to 6 pieces of chicken (thighs, drumsticks, or a mix)
- 2 tablespoons extra virgin olive oil
- 1 onion, chopped
- 3 cloves garlic, minced
- 1 red bell pepper, sliced
- 1 yellow bell pepper, sliced
- 1 can (28 ounces) crushed tomatoes
- 1/2 cup red wine (optional)
- 1 teaspoon dried oregano
- 1 teaspoon dried thyme
- 1 bay leaf
- Salt and pepper to taste
- Fresh basil leaves for garnish
- Grated Parmesan cheese for serving (optional)

Instructions:
Step 1: Prepare the Chicken

1. Start by seasoning the chicken pieces with salt and pepper. This

will enhance the flavor of the chicken as it cooks.

Step 2: Sauté the Aromatics

1. In a large skillet or Dutch oven, heat the olive oil over medium-high heat. Add the chopped onion and sauté until it becomes translucent, about 3 minutes.
2. Add the minced garlic and sauté for another 30 seconds until fragrant.

Step 3: Brown the Chicken

1. Push the sautéed onion and garlic to the side of the skillet, making space in the center. Place the chicken pieces in the center of the skillet, skin-side down.
2. Allow the chicken to brown for about 5 minutes on each side, until it develops a golden-brown crust. This step adds depth of flavor to the dish.

Step 4: Create the Tomato Sauce

1. Pour in the crushed tomatoes, red wine (if using), dried oregano, dried thyme, and bay leaf. Stir everything together to combine.
2. Reduce the heat to low, cover the skillet, and let the sauce simmer gently for about 30-40 minutes. This slow simmer allows the chicken to become tender and absorbs the rich flavors of the sauce.

Step 5: Add Bell Peppers

1. After the chicken has simmered for about 20 minutes, add the sliced red and yellow bell peppers to the skillet. Continue to

simmer uncovered for the remaining 20 minutes.

Step 6: Serve and Garnish

1. Once the chicken is tender and cooked through, remove the bay leaf.
2. Serve your Traditional Italian Chicken Cacciatore hot, garnished with fresh basil leaves. Optionally, you can sprinkle grated Parmesan cheese on top for an extra burst of flavor.

Pairing Suggestions and Wine Recommendations

To complement the robust flavors of Traditional Italian Chicken Cacciatore, consider these pairing suggestions:

Pasta: Serve your Chicken Cacciatore over al dente spaghetti, linguine, or fettuccine for a hearty and satisfying meal.

Polenta: Creamy polenta provides a wonderful base for the savory chicken and tomato sauce.

Crusty Bread: A loaf of fresh, crusty Italian bread is perfect for mopping up the delicious sauce.

With this classic recipe in your repertoire, you're well on your way to becoming a Chicken Cacciatore connoisseur. In the following chapters, we'll explore creative variations and modern twists on this Italian favorite, so stay tuned for more culinary adventures!

Chapter 3: Rustic Vegetable Cacciatore

A Vegetarian Twist on the Italian Classic

In this chapter, we'll take a delightful detour from the traditional Chicken Cacciatore and explore the world of Rustic Vegetable Cacciatore. This vegetarian twist on the Italian classic is perfect for those looking to savor the rich flavors of Cacciatore without the meat. It's a celebration of seasonal vegetables and the same aromatic, tomato-based sauce that makes Chicken Cacciatore so beloved.

Ingredients:

- 2 tablespoons extra virgin olive oil
- 1 onion, chopped
- 3 cloves garlic, minced
- 1 red bell pepper, sliced
- 1 yellow bell pepper, sliced
- 1 zucchini, sliced
- 1 eggplant, diced
- 1 can (28 ounces) crushed tomatoes
- 1/2 cup vegetable broth
- 1 teaspoon dried oregano
- 1 teaspoon dried thyme
- 1 bay leaf
- Salt and pepper to taste
- Fresh basil leaves for garnish
- Grated Parmesan cheese for serving (optional)

Instructions:

Step 1: Sauté the Aromatics

1. In a large skillet or Dutch oven, heat the olive oil over medium-

high heat. Add the chopped onion and sauté until it becomes translucent, about 3 minutes.

2. Add the minced garlic and sauté for another 30 seconds until fragrant.

Step 2: Add the Vegetables

1. Incorporate the sliced red and yellow bell peppers, zucchini, and diced eggplant into the skillet. Sauté the vegetables for about 5-7 minutes until they begin to soften.

Step 3: Create the Tomato Sauce

1. Pour in the crushed tomatoes, vegetable broth, dried oregano, dried thyme, and bay leaf. Stir everything together to combine.
2. Reduce the heat to low, cover the skillet, and let the sauce simmer gently for about 20-25 minutes. This allows the vegetables to become tender and absorb the flavors of the sauce.

Step 4: Serve and Garnish

1. Once the vegetables are tender and cooked through, remove the bay leaf.
2. Serve your Rustic Vegetable Cacciatore hot, garnished with fresh basil leaves. Optionally, you can sprinkle grated Parmesan cheese on top for added richness.

Variations with Seasonal Vegetables

The beauty of Rustic Vegetable Cacciatore lies in its versatility. You can adapt this dish to suit the seasons and take advantage of the freshest produce available. Here are some seasonal variations to consider:

Spring: Asparagus, peas, and artichokes can be wonderful additions in the spring. Their bright, fresh flavors complement the tomato sauce beautifully.

Summer: In the peak of summer, incorporate cherry tomatoes, summer squash, and fresh basil for a burst of seasonal goodness.

Fall: Root vegetables like carrots, butternut squash, and Brussels sprouts add depth and earthiness to your autumn-inspired Cacciatore.

Winter: Roasted winter vegetables, such as sweet potatoes and cauliflower, can create a comforting winter variation.

Rustic Vegetable Cacciatore is a celebration of the bountiful produce that each season brings. Experiment with different vegetables and find your favorite combinations to suit the time of year.

With this vegetarian twist on Cacciatore, you're not only enjoying a delicious and hearty meal but also embracing the beauty of seasonal cooking. In the upcoming chapters, we'll explore even more creative variations of this Italian classic, so stay tuned for more culinary inspiration!

Chapter 4: Chicken Cacciatore with a Twist

Creative Variations and Fusion Recipes

In this chapter, we're taking the classic Chicken Cacciatore and giving it a modern twist. We'll explore creative variations and fusion recipes that incorporate different cuisines and flavors, elevating this beloved Italian dish to new heights. Get ready to embark on a culinary adventure that combines the traditional with the innovative.

1. Mediterranean-Inspired Chicken Cacciatore

Ingredients:

- 4 to 6 pieces of chicken (thighs, drumsticks, or a mix)
- 2 tablespoons extra virgin olive oil
- 1 onion, chopped
- 3 cloves garlic, minced
- 1 red bell pepper, sliced
- 1 yellow bell pepper, sliced
- 1 can (14 ounces) artichoke hearts, drained and quartered
- 1/2 cup Kalamata olives, pitted
- 1 can (14 ounces) diced tomatoes with Mediterranean herbs
- 1/2 cup white wine
- 1 teaspoon dried oregano
- 1 teaspoon dried thyme
- Salt and pepper to taste
- Feta cheese crumbles for garnish

Instructions:

1. Follow the same cooking steps as outlined in Chapter 2 for the classic Chicken Cacciatore recipe, but incorporate the artichoke hearts and Kalamata olives when you add the bell

peppers.

2. After removing the bay leaf, serve your Mediterranean-Inspired Chicken Cacciatore hot, garnished with crumbled feta cheese. This variation combines the flavors of the Mediterranean with the Italian classic.

2. Asian Fusion Chicken Cacciatore
Ingredients:

- 4 to 6 pieces of chicken (thighs, drumsticks, or a mix)
- 2 tablespoons sesame oil
- 1 onion, chopped
- 3 cloves garlic, minced
- 1 red bell pepper, sliced
- 1 yellow bell pepper, sliced
- 1 cup shiitake mushrooms, sliced
- 1 can (14 ounces) diced tomatoes with ginger and soy sauce
- 1/2 cup chicken broth
- 2 tablespoons soy sauce
- 1 tablespoon hoisin sauce
- 1 teaspoon Chinese five-spice powder
- Green onions for garnish

Instructions:

1. Follow the same cooking steps as outlined in Chapter 2 for the classic Chicken Cacciatore recipe, but use sesame oil instead of olive oil and incorporate the shiitake mushrooms when you add the bell peppers.

1. After removing the bay leaf, serve your Asian Fusion Chicken Cacciatore hot, garnished with sliced green onions. This fusion dish combines Italian and Asian flavors for a unique and delicious experience.

3. Tex-Mex Chicken Cacciatore
Ingredients:

- 4 to 6 pieces of chicken (thighs, drumsticks, or a mix)
- 2 tablespoons vegetable oil
- 1 onion, chopped
- 3 cloves garlic, minced
- 1 red bell pepper, sliced
- 1 yellow bell pepper, sliced
- 1 can (14 ounces) diced tomatoes with green chilies
- 1/2 cup chicken broth
- 1 teaspoon chili powder
- 1 teaspoon cumin
- Salt and pepper to taste
- Fresh cilantro leaves for garnish
- Sour cream for serving (optional)

Instructions:

1. Follow the same cooking steps as outlined in Chapter 2 for the classic Chicken Cacciatore recipe, but use vegetable oil instead of olive oil and incorporate the diced tomatoes with green chilies when you add the bell peppers.
2. After removing the bay leaf, serve your Tex-Mex Chicken Cacciatore hot, garnished with fresh cilantro leaves. For a creamy twist, add a dollop of sour cream before serving.

These creative variations of Chicken Cacciatore demonstrate the adaptability of this dish and its ability to blend flavors from around the world. Feel free to experiment with different ingredients and cuisines to create your own unique twists on this Italian classic.

Chapter 5: Slow Cooker and Instant Pot Chicken Cacciatore

Easy and Convenient Cooking Methods

In this chapter, we'll explore two time-saving and convenient methods for preparing Chicken Cacciatore: the slow cooker and the Instant Pot. Whether you have a busy schedule or simply prefer a set-it-and-forget-it approach, these cooking techniques will help you create a delicious meal with minimal effort.

Slow Cooker Chicken Cacciatore

Ingredients:

- 4 to 6 pieces of chicken (thighs, drumsticks, or a mix)
- 2 tablespoons extra virgin olive oil
- 1 onion, chopped
- 3 cloves garlic, minced
- 1 red bell pepper, sliced
- 1 yellow bell pepper, sliced
- 1 can (28 ounces) crushed tomatoes
- 1/2 cup red wine (optional)
- 1 teaspoon dried oregano
- 1 teaspoon dried thyme
- 1 bay leaf
- Salt and pepper to taste
- Fresh basil leaves for garnish
- Grated Parmesan cheese for serving (optional)

Instructions:

1. Season the chicken pieces with salt and pepper.
2. In a skillet, heat the olive oil over medium-high heat. Sauté the chopped onion and minced garlic until the onion becomes

translucent.

3. Add the sliced red and yellow bell peppers and sauté for another 3-5 minutes until they begin to soften.
4. Transfer the sautéed ingredients to your slow cooker.
5. Place the seasoned chicken pieces on top of the sautéed vegetables.
6. Pour in the crushed tomatoes, red wine (if using), dried oregano, dried thyme, and add the bay leaf. Stir everything to combine.
7. Cover the slow cooker and cook on the low setting for 6-8 hours or on the high setting for 3-4 hours, until the chicken is tender and cooked through.
8. Remove the bay leaf before serving.
9. Serve your Slow Cooker Chicken Cacciatore hot, garnished with fresh basil leaves. Optionally, you can sprinkle grated Parmesan cheese on top for added richness.

Instant Pot Chicken Cacciatore
Ingredients:

- 4 to 6 pieces of chicken (thighs, drumsticks, or a mix)
- 2 tablespoons extra virgin olive oil
- 1 onion, chopped
- 3 cloves garlic, minced
- 1 red bell pepper, sliced
- 1 yellow bell pepper, sliced
- 1 can (28 ounces) crushed tomatoes
- 1/2 cup red wine (optional)
- 1 teaspoon dried oregano
- 1 teaspoon dried thyme
- 1 bay leaf

- Salt and pepper to taste
- Fresh basil leaves for garnish
- Grated Parmesan cheese for serving (optional)

Instructions:

1. Set your Instant Pot to the "Sauté" function. Heat the olive oil in the pot and sauté the chopped onion and minced garlic until the onion becomes translucent.
2. Add the sliced red and yellow bell peppers and sauté for another 3-5 minutes until they begin to soften.
3. Season the chicken pieces with salt and pepper.
4. Place the seasoned chicken pieces on top of the sautéed vegetables in the Instant Pot.
5. Pour in the crushed tomatoes, red wine (if using), dried oregano, dried thyme, and add the bay leaf. Stir everything to combine.
6. Close the Instant Pot lid, set the vent to "Sealing," and select the "Pressure Cook" function. Cook on high pressure for 15 minutes.
7. Once the cooking cycle is complete, allow for a natural release of pressure for about 10 minutes before carefully venting the remaining pressure.
8. Remove the bay leaf before serving.
9. Serve your Instant Pot Chicken Cacciatore hot, garnished with fresh basil leaves. Optionally, you can sprinkle grated Parmesan cheese on top for added richness.

These cooking methods make preparing Chicken Cacciatore a breeze, allowing you to enjoy the flavors of Italy with minimal effort.

Chapter 6: Healthy Chicken Cacciatore

Lighter Versions with Reduced Fat and Calories

In this chapter, we'll explore how to make Chicken Cacciatore a healthier option without compromising on flavor. By making some strategic ingredient swaps and cooking choices, you can enjoy this Italian classic while reducing fat and calories. We'll also discuss the nutritional benefits and dietary considerations of these healthier variations.

Ingredients for Healthy Chicken Cacciatore:

- 4 to 6 pieces of chicken (boneless, skinless chicken breasts or thighs)
- 2 teaspoons olive oil
- 1 onion, chopped
- 3 cloves garlic, minced
- 1 red bell pepper, sliced
- 1 yellow bell pepper, sliced
- 1 can (14 ounces) diced tomatoes (no added salt)
- 1/2 cup low-sodium chicken broth
- 1 teaspoon dried oregano
- 1 teaspoon dried thyme
- Salt and pepper to taste
- Fresh basil leaves for garnish
- Grated Parmesan cheese (optional, use sparingly)

Cooking Instructions:

Step 1: Sautéing with Less Oil

1. Heat the olive oil in a skillet over medium heat. Use a non-stick skillet to minimize the need for excess oil.
2. Add the chopped onion and sauté until it becomes translucent,

about 3 minutes.

3. Add the minced garlic and sauté for another 30 seconds until fragrant.

Step 2: Using Lean Chicken

1. Season the boneless, skinless chicken pieces with salt and pepper. Boneless, skinless chicken breasts or thighs are lower in fat and calories compared to traditional cuts.

Step 3: Incorporating Vegetables and Tomatoes

1. Add the sliced red and yellow bell peppers to the skillet and sauté for about 5 minutes until they begin to soften.
2. Stir in the diced tomatoes and low-sodium chicken broth.
3. Season with dried oregano and dried thyme for flavor without added calories.

Step 4: Cooking and Serving

1. Add the seasoned chicken pieces to the skillet, making sure they are evenly distributed.
2. Cover the skillet and let the dish simmer gently for about 15-20 minutes until the chicken is cooked through and the sauce has thickened.
3. Remove from heat, and season with additional salt and pepper if needed.
4. Serve your Healthy Chicken Cacciatore hot, garnished with fresh basil leaves. If you'd like, add a small amount of grated Parmesan cheese for a touch of richness, but use it sparingly to keep the dish healthy.

Nutritional Benefits and Dietary Considerations

Lean Protein: Boneless, skinless chicken provides lean protein, which is essential for muscle maintenance and repair.

Low in Saturated Fat: By using lean chicken cuts and minimal oil, this version of Chicken Cacciatore is lower in saturated fat, making it heart-healthy.

Fiber and Vitamins: Bell peppers and tomatoes are rich in fiber, vitamins, and antioxidants, promoting overall health.

Low Sodium Option: Opting for no-salt-added diced tomatoes and low-sodium chicken broth reduces the dish's sodium content, important for those with dietary restrictions.

Gluten-Free: This recipe is naturally gluten-free, making it suitable for individuals with gluten sensitivities.

Calorie Control: By being mindful of portion sizes and cheese use, you can control calorie intake while enjoying a satisfying meal.

Healthy Chicken Cacciatore proves that you can indulge in comfort food while making choices that align with your health and dietary goals. In the upcoming chapters, we'll continue to explore different variations of this classic dish, catering to a variety of tastes and preferences.

Chapter 7: One-Pot Chicken Cacciatore

Simplified Cooking for Busy Days

In this chapter, we'll explore a hassle-free method of making Chicken Cacciatore that's perfect for those busy days when you want a delicious meal without a sink full of dishes. One-Pot Chicken Cacciatore streamlines the cooking process while ensuring that cleanup is a breeze. It's the ultimate recipe for simplicity and convenience.

Ingredients for One-Pot Chicken Cacciatore:

- 4 to 6 pieces of chicken (thighs, drumsticks, or a mix)
- 2 tablespoons extra virgin olive oil
- 1 onion, chopped
- 3 cloves garlic, minced
- 1 red bell pepper, sliced
- 1 yellow bell pepper, sliced
- 1 can (28 ounces) crushed tomatoes
- 1/2 cup red wine (optional)
- 1 teaspoon dried oregano
- 1 teaspoon dried thyme
- 1 bay leaf
- Salt and pepper to taste
- Fresh basil leaves for garnish
- Grated Parmesan cheese for serving (optional)

Cooking Instructions:

Step 1: Sautéing and Searing

1. In a large, oven-safe skillet or Dutch oven, heat the olive oil over medium-high heat. This will be your one-pot wonder, so choose a vessel that can go from stovetop to oven.

2. Add the chopped onion and sauté until it becomes translucent, about 3 minutes.
3. Add the minced garlic and sauté for another 30 seconds until fragrant.
4. Push the sautéed onion and garlic to the side of the skillet, creating space in the center. Place the chicken pieces in the center, skin-side down, and sear them until they develop a golden-brown crust, about 5 minutes on each side.

Step 2: Assembling the Dish

1. Once the chicken is nicely seared, add the sliced red and yellow bell peppers to the skillet.
2. Pour in the crushed tomatoes, red wine (if using), dried oregano, dried thyme, and add the bay leaf. Stir everything together to combine.

Step 3: Simmering and Finishing

1. Reduce the heat to low, cover the skillet or Dutch oven, and let the dish simmer gently for about 30-40 minutes. This will allow the chicken to become tender and absorb the rich flavors of the sauce.
2. Preheat your oven to 350°F (175°C).
3. Remove the bay leaf from the skillet.
4. Transfer the skillet or Dutch oven to the preheated oven and bake, uncovered, for an additional 15-20 minutes to ensure the chicken is cooked through.

Step 4: Serving and Cleanup

1. Serve your One-Pot Chicken Cacciatore hot, garnished with fresh basil leaves. Optionally, you can sprinkle grated Parmesan cheese on top for added richness.

2. Enjoy your meal, knowing that cleanup is a breeze because you've used just one pot for both cooking and serving.

One-Pot Chicken Cacciatore is a lifesaver on busy days when you crave a comforting, homemade meal but don't want the fuss of dealing with multiple dishes. It's a time-efficient and delicious solution for your culinary needs.

Chapter 8: Grilled Chicken Cacciatore

Bringing the Outdoors into Your Kitchen

In this chapter, we'll explore a unique and flavorful way to prepare Chicken Cacciatore—on the grill! Grilled Chicken Cacciatore brings the smoky essence of outdoor cooking into your kitchen, infusing the dish with a delicious charred flavor. We'll also delve into marinades and grilling techniques to make your culinary adventure a success.

Ingredients for Grilled Chicken Cacciatore:

- 4 to 6 pieces of chicken (thighs, drumsticks, or a mix)
- 2 tablespoons extra virgin olive oil
- 1 onion, chopped
- 3 cloves garlic, minced
- 1 red bell pepper, sliced
- 1 yellow bell pepper, sliced
- 1 can (14 ounces) fire-roasted diced tomatoes
- 1/2 cup red wine (optional)
- 1 teaspoon dried oregano
- 1 teaspoon dried thyme
- Salt and pepper to taste
- Fresh basil leaves for garnish
- Grated Parmesan cheese for serving (optional)

Marinade for Grilled Chicken:

- 1/4 cup extra virgin olive oil
- 2 tablespoons balsamic vinegar
- 1 tablespoon Dijon mustard
- 2 cloves garlic, minced
- 1 teaspoon dried Italian herbs (basil, oregano, thyme)
- Salt and pepper to taste

Grilling Instructions:
Step 1: Preparing the Marinade

1. In a small bowl, whisk together the olive oil, balsamic vinegar, Dijon mustard, minced garlic, and dried Italian herbs. Season with salt and pepper to taste.
2. Place the chicken pieces in a resealable plastic bag or shallow dish and pour the marinade over them. Seal the bag or cover the dish and refrigerate for at least 30 minutes, or ideally, for a few hours to allow the flavors to meld.

Step 2: Grilling the Chicken

1. Preheat your grill to medium-high heat (around 400°F or 200°C) and oil the grates to prevent sticking.
2. Remove the chicken from the marinade, allowing any excess to drip off.
3. Grill the chicken pieces over direct heat, skin-side down, for about 5-7 minutes per side, or until they have a nice char and are cooked through.

Step 3: Preparing the Sauce

1. While the chicken is grilling, you can prepare the sauce indoors. In a skillet, heat the olive oil over medium-high heat.
2. Sauté the chopped onion until it becomes translucent, about 3 minutes.
3. Add the minced garlic and sauté for another 30 seconds until fragrant.
4. Add the sliced red and yellow bell peppers and sauté for about 5 minutes until they begin to soften.
5. Stir in the fire-roasted diced tomatoes, red wine (if using), dried oregano, and dried thyme. Season with salt and pepper.
6. Simmer the sauce for 10-15 minutes to allow the flavors to

meld.

Step 4: Serving

1. Remove the grilled chicken from the grill and place it on a serving platter.
2. Spoon the prepared sauce over the grilled chicken.
3. Garnish with fresh basil leaves and, if desired, sprinkle with grated Parmesan cheese for added richness.

Grilled Chicken Cacciatore is a delightful fusion of outdoor grilling and classic Italian flavors. The marinade infuses the chicken with a burst of taste, while the grill imparts a smoky char that adds depth to the dish.

Chapter 9: Chicken Cacciatore for Entertaining

Impress Your Guests with Elegant Variations

In this chapter, we'll elevate Chicken Cacciatore to a gourmet level, perfect for impressing your guests during special occasions and dinner parties. We'll explore elegant variations of this classic dish and provide plating and presentation tips to ensure your Chicken Cacciatore not only tastes divine but looks like a work of art on the plate.

Ingredients for Elegant Chicken Cacciatore:

- 4 to 6 pieces of chicken (bone-in, skin-on chicken thighs or drumsticks)
- 2 tablespoons extra virgin olive oil
- 1 onion, finely chopped
- 3 cloves garlic, minced
- 1 red bell pepper, thinly sliced
- 1 yellow bell pepper, thinly sliced
- 1 cup mixed mushrooms (shiitake, cremini, or wild mushrooms), sliced
- 1 can (14 ounces) crushed San Marzano tomatoes
- 1/2 cup dry white wine
- 1 teaspoon dried oregano
- 1 teaspoon dried thyme
- Salt and freshly ground black pepper to taste
- Fresh basil leaves for garnish
- Shaved Parmesan cheese for serving (optional)

Plating and Presentation Tips:

Individual Servings: Consider serving each guest an individual portion of Chicken Cacciatore on a well-plated dish. This adds a touch of elegance and ensures consistent presentation.

Gourmet Plating: Use a circular mold or a small ramekin to shape a portion of creamy polenta or mashed potatoes at the center of each plate. Place the Chicken Cacciatore over the polenta or potatoes for an upscale presentation.

Garnish with Microgreens: Sprinkle a handful of fresh microgreens, such as arugula or basil microgreens, over the Chicken Cacciatore just before serving. They add a pop of color and a delicate flavor.

Drizzle of High-Quality Olive Oil: Right before serving, lightly drizzle each plate with a high-quality extra virgin olive oil. The fruity notes of the oil will enhance the dish's flavors and add a luxurious touch.

Freshly Shaved Parmesan: For a final flourish, use a vegetable peeler to shave thin, delicate curls of Parmesan cheese over each serving. This adds both texture and an exquisite flavor.

Cooking Instructions for Elegant Chicken Cacciatore:
Step 1: Sautéing and Browning

1. In a large skillet or sauté pan, heat the olive oil over medium-high heat.
2. Sauté the finely chopped onion until it becomes translucent, about 3 minutes.
3. Add the minced garlic and sauté for another 30 seconds until fragrant.
4. Add the thinly sliced red and yellow bell peppers, as well as the mixed mushrooms, to the skillet. Sauté for about 5-7 minutes until they begin to caramelize.

Step 2: Preparing the Chicken and Sauce

1. Season the bone-in, skin-on chicken pieces with salt and freshly ground black pepper.

2. Push the sautéed vegetables to the side of the skillet, creating space in the center. Place the seasoned chicken pieces in the center, skin-side down.
3. Allow the chicken to sear and develop a golden-brown crust, about 5 minutes on each side.
4. Pour in the crushed San Marzano tomatoes, dry white wine, dried oregano, and dried thyme. Stir everything together to combine.
5. Reduce the heat to low, cover the skillet, and let the dish simmer gently for about 30-40 minutes until the chicken is tender and the sauce has thickened.

Step 3: Serving with Elegance

1. Assemble each plate by placing a circular mold or a small ramekin of creamy polenta or mashed potatoes at the center.
2. Carefully arrange a piece of seared chicken on top of the polenta or potatoes.
3. Spoon the rich, flavorful sauce, along with the sautéed vegetables, over the chicken and around the plate.
4. Garnish with fresh basil leaves, shaved Parmesan cheese, a drizzle of high-quality olive oil, and a sprinkle of microgreens.

Elegant Chicken Cacciatore is a showstopper that combines the rustic charm of the Italian classic with gourmet presentation. Your guests will be delighted by the flavors and impressed by the visual appeal.

Chapter 10: International Cacciatore Flavors

Exploring Global Interpretations of the Dish

In this chapter, we'll take a culinary journey around the world and explore how different cultures have interpreted the concept of Cacciatore. Each region brings its own unique flavors and ingredients to this beloved dish, resulting in a diverse array of delicious recipes.

Italian Chicken Cacciatore (Classic)

Ingredients:

- 4 to 6 pieces of chicken (thighs, drumsticks, or a mix)
- 2 tablespoons extra virgin olive oil
- 1 onion, chopped
- 3 cloves garlic, minced
- 1 red bell pepper, sliced
- 1 yellow bell pepper, sliced
- 1 can (28 ounces) crushed tomatoes
- 1/2 cup red wine (optional)
- 1 teaspoon dried oregano
- 1 teaspoon dried thyme
- Salt and pepper to taste
- Fresh basil leaves for garnish
- Grated Parmesan cheese for serving (optional)

Instructions:

1. Follow the cooking instructions outlined in Chapter 2 for the classic Italian Chicken Cacciatore.

Spanish Chicken Cacciatore (Pollo a la Cazadora)

Ingredients:

- 4 to 6 pieces of chicken (thighs, drumsticks, or a mix)
- 2 tablespoons olive oil
- 1 onion, chopped
- 2 cloves garlic, minced
- 1 red bell pepper, sliced
- 1 green bell pepper, sliced
- 1 cup white wine
- 1 can (14 ounces) diced tomatoes
- 1 teaspoon smoked paprika (pimentón)
- 1 teaspoon dried thyme
- Salt and pepper to taste
- Fresh parsley for garnish

Instructions:

1. In a large skillet or Dutch oven, follow the same cooking steps as outlined in Chapter 2 for the classic Italian Chicken Cacciatore, but replace red wine with white wine and add smoked paprika for a Spanish twist.

French Chicken Cacciatore (Poulet Chasseur)
Ingredients:

- 4 to 6 pieces of chicken (thighs, drumsticks, or a mix)
- 2 tablespoons butter
- 1 onion, chopped
- 1 shallot, minced
- 8 ounces mushrooms, sliced
- 1/2 cup dry white wine
- 1 can (14 ounces) diced tomatoes
- 1/2 cup chicken broth

- 2 teaspoons fresh tarragon, chopped
- Salt and pepper to taste
- Fresh chives for garnish

Instructions:

1. In a large skillet or Dutch oven, melt the butter over medium-high heat. Follow the same cooking steps as outlined in Chapter 2 for the classic Italian Chicken Cacciatore, but replace olive oil with butter, add minced shallot, and incorporate fresh tarragon for a French flair.

Greek Chicken Cacciatore
Ingredients:

- 4 to 6 pieces of chicken (thighs, drumsticks, or a mix)
- 2 tablespoons extra virgin olive oil
- 1 onion, chopped
- 3 cloves garlic, minced
- 1 red bell pepper, sliced
- 1 yellow bell pepper, sliced
- 1 can (14 ounces) diced tomatoes with Mediterranean herbs
- 1/2 cup Kalamata olives, pitted
- 2 tablespoons fresh lemon juice
- 1 teaspoon dried oregano
- Salt and pepper to taste
- Fresh parsley for garnish
- Feta cheese crumbles for serving (optional)

Instructions:

1. In a large skillet or Dutch oven, follow the same cooking steps as outlined in Chapter 2 for the classic Italian Chicken Cacciatore, but incorporate Kalamata olives, fresh lemon juice, and use diced tomatoes with Mediterranean herbs for a Greek twist.

Thai Chicken Cacciatore (Gai Phad Cha)
Ingredients:

- 4 to 6 pieces of chicken (thighs, drumsticks, or a mix)
- 2 tablespoons vegetable oil
- 1 onion, chopped
- 2 cloves garlic, minced
- 2 Thai bird's eye chilies, finely chopped (adjust to taste)
- 1 red bell pepper, sliced
- 1 green bell pepper, sliced
- 1 can (14 ounces) coconut milk
- 2 tablespoons fish sauce
- 1 tablespoon soy sauce
- 1 teaspoon sugar
- Fresh Thai basil leaves for garnish
- Jasmine rice for serving

Instructions:

In a wok or large skillet, heat the vegetable oil over medium-high heat. Follow the same cooking steps as outlined in Chapter 2 for the classic Italian Chicken Cacciatore, but replace the tomato-based sauce with coconut milk, and incorporate Thai bird's eye chilies, fish sauce, soy sauce, and sugar for a Thai-inspired version.

These international variations of Chicken Cacciatore showcase the incredible diversity of flavors and ingredients that can be incorporated into this beloved dish. Whether you're in the mood for Spanish, French, Greek, or Thai flavors, there's a Chicken Cacciatore recipe for every culinary adventure.

Chapter 11: Chicken Cacciatore for Kids

Family-Friendly Versions and Kid-Approved Recipes

In this chapter, we'll cater to the younger generation and create family-friendly versions of Chicken Cacciatore that kids will love. We'll also explore fun ways to get children involved in the cooking process, making it an enjoyable and educational experience for the whole family.

Kid-Approved Chicken Cacciatore Recipe:

Ingredients:

- 4 to 6 pieces of chicken (boneless, skinless chicken breasts or thighs)
- 2 tablespoons olive oil
- 1 onion, finely chopped
- 2 cloves garlic, minced
- 1 red bell pepper, diced
- 1 yellow bell pepper, diced
- 1 can (14 ounces) diced tomatoes (no added salt)
- 1/2 cup low-sodium chicken broth
- 1 teaspoon dried oregano
- 1 teaspoon dried thyme
- Salt and pepper to taste
- 1 cup cooked pasta (such as penne or spaghetti)
- Fresh basil leaves for garnish (optional)
- Grated Parmesan cheese for serving (optional)

Instructions:

Step 1: Sautéing with Care

1. In a large skillet, heat the olive oil over medium heat.
2. Add the finely chopped onion and sauté until it becomes translucent, about 3 minutes.

3. Add the minced garlic and sauté for another 30 seconds until fragrant.

4. Add the diced red and yellow bell peppers and sauté for about 5 minutes until they begin to soften.

Step 2: Cooking with Kids

1. Involve your children in the cooking process by having them help measure and add the dried oregano and dried thyme to the skillet. Explain the importance of herbs in flavoring dishes.

2. If age-appropriate, allow them to safely stir the ingredients in the skillet under supervision.

Step 3: Simmering and Serving

1. Add the boneless, skinless chicken pieces to the skillet and season with salt and pepper.

2. Pour in the diced tomatoes and low-sodium chicken broth. Stir everything together.

3. Cover the skillet and let the dish simmer gently for about 15-20 minutes until the chicken is cooked through.

4. Serve the Kid-Approved Chicken Cacciatore over cooked pasta. Garnish with fresh basil leaves (if available) and offer grated Parmesan cheese on the side for children to sprinkle on their portions.

Getting Kids Involved:
Fun with Ingredients:
Encourage your kids to help with age-appropriate tasks like washing vegetables, measuring ingredients, and stirring.

Teach them about different ingredients and their flavors. Let them taste and smell herbs, spices, and vegetables to understand their role in cooking.

Creative Plating:

Make mealtime fun by allowing your kids to arrange their Chicken Cacciatore and pasta on the plate in creative ways. They can create smiley faces or patterns with the food.

Taste Testing:

Involve your children in taste testing. Ask them to describe the flavors they taste and express their preferences. It's a great way to develop their palates.

Cooking Games:

Turn cooking into a game by timing tasks or challenging your kids to find ingredients in the pantry. Cooking can be both educational and entertaining.

Kid-Approved Chicken Cacciatore is designed to be delicious, nutritious, and enjoyable for the entire family. It's a wonderful opportunity to bond with your children in the kitchen and instill a love for cooking and good food from a young age.

Chapter 12: Gluten-Free Chicken Cacciatore

Safe and Delicious Options for Gluten-Sensitive Individuals

In this chapter, we'll explore how to make Chicken Cacciatore safe and delicious for individuals with gluten sensitivities or those following a gluten-free diet. We'll also delve into gluten-free flour substitutes and recipes to help you achieve the same comforting flavors without the gluten.

Gluten-Free Chicken Cacciatore Recipe:

Ingredients:

- 4 to 6 pieces of chicken (thighs, drumsticks, or a mix)
- 2 tablespoons olive oil
- 1 onion, chopped
- 3 cloves garlic, minced
- 1 red bell pepper, sliced
- 1 yellow bell pepper, sliced
- 1 can (14 ounces) diced tomatoes (gluten-free, no added salt)
- 1/2 cup gluten-free chicken broth
- 1 teaspoon dried oregano
- 1 teaspoon dried thyme
- Salt and pepper to taste
- Fresh basil leaves for garnish (optional)
- Grated Parmesan cheese (use a certified gluten-free brand, optional)
- Gluten-free pasta (such as rice pasta or corn pasta)

Instructions:

Step 1: Sautéing and Browning

1. In a large skillet, heat the olive oil over medium-high heat.

2. Add the chopped onion and sauté until it becomes translucent, about 3 minutes.
3. Add the minced garlic and sauté for another 30 seconds until fragrant.
4. Add the sliced red and yellow bell peppers to the skillet and sauté for about 5-7 minutes until they begin to soften.

Step 2: Gluten-Free Flour Substitute

1. To thicken the sauce without gluten, you can use a gluten-free flour substitute. In a small bowl, mix 2 tablespoons of cornstarch or a gluten-free flour blend with 1/4 cup of cold water until it forms a smooth slurry.
2. Add the slurry to the skillet and stir it into the sautéed vegetables. This will help thicken the sauce as it simmers.

Step 3: Preparing the Chicken and Sauce

1. Season the chicken pieces with salt and pepper.
2. Push the sautéed vegetables to the side of the skillet, creating space in the center. Place the seasoned chicken pieces in the center.
3. Allow the chicken to sear and develop a golden-brown crust, about 5 minutes on each side.
4. Pour in the diced tomatoes and gluten-free chicken broth. Stir everything together.

Step 4: Simmering and Serving

1. Cover the skillet and let the dish simmer gently for about 15-20 minutes until the chicken is cooked through and the sauce has thickened.
2. While the Chicken Cacciatore is simmering, cook gluten-free pasta according to the package instructions.

3. Serve the Gluten-Free Chicken Cacciatore hot, garnished with fresh basil leaves (if available). Offer grated Parmesan cheese on the side for those who prefer it.

Gluten-Free Flour Substitutes:

Cornstarch:

Cornstarch is a gluten-free thickening agent commonly used in recipes. It creates a smooth, glossy sauce.

Gluten-Free Flour Blends:

Many certified gluten-free flour blends are available in stores. They are designed to mimic the properties of wheat flour in recipes.

Look for blends made from rice flour, tapioca starch, potato starch, and xanthan gum.

Experiment with different brands and blends to find your favorite for gluten-free cooking.

Gluten-Free Chicken Cacciatore is a safe and delicious option for individuals with gluten sensitivities or those following a gluten-free diet. By using gluten-free pasta and a suitable flour substitute, you can enjoy this classic Italian dish without compromise.

Chapter 13: Spicy Chicken Cacciatore

Adding a Kick to Your Favorite Dish

In this chapter, we'll turn up the heat and add a fiery twist to the classic Chicken Cacciatore. Spicy Chicken Cacciatore incorporates pepper and spice variations to create a dish that's bold, flavorful, and sure to satisfy those who crave a bit of heat in their meals.

Ingredients for Spicy Chicken Cacciatore:

- 4 to 6 pieces of chicken (thighs, drumsticks, or a mix)
- 2 tablespoons olive oil
- 1 onion, chopped
- 3 cloves garlic, minced
- 1 red bell pepper, sliced
- 1 yellow bell pepper, sliced
- 1 can (14 ounces) diced tomatoes with green chilies
- 1/2 cup chicken broth
- 1 teaspoon crushed red pepper flakes (adjust to taste)
- 1 teaspoon smoked paprika
- Salt and pepper to taste
- Fresh cilantro leaves for garnish (optional)
- Jalapeño slices for extra heat (optional)

Pepper and Spice Variations:
Crushed Red Pepper Flakes:
Crushed red pepper flakes add a moderate level of heat to the dish. Adjust the amount to your preferred spice level.

Jalapeño Slices:
For those who love extra heat, garnish the Spicy Chicken Cacciatore with thin slices of fresh jalapeño peppers.

Chipotle Peppers in Adobo Sauce:
If you desire a smoky and intense heat, consider adding minced chipotle peppers in adobo sauce to the sauce mixture. Start with one or two peppers, as they can be quite spicy.

Instructions:
Step 1: Sautéing and Browning

1. In a large skillet, heat the olive oil over medium-high heat.
2. Add the chopped onion and sauté until it becomes translucent, about 3 minutes.
3. Add the minced garlic and sauté for another 30 seconds until fragrant.
4. Add the sliced red and yellow bell peppers to the skillet and sauté for about 5-7 minutes until they begin to soften.

Step 2: Spicing It Up

1. Season the chicken pieces with salt and pepper.
2. Push the sautéed vegetables to the side of the skillet, creating space in the center. Place the seasoned chicken pieces in the center.
3. Allow the chicken to sear and develop a golden-brown crust, about 5 minutes on each side.
4. Add the diced tomatoes with green chilies, chicken broth, crushed red pepper flakes, and smoked paprika. Stir everything together.

Step 3: Simmering and Serving

1. Cover the skillet and let the dish simmer gently for about 15-20 minutes until the chicken is cooked through.
2. Taste and adjust the heat level by adding more crushed red pepper flakes or jalapeño slices if desired.
3. Serve the Spicy Chicken Cacciatore hot, garnished with fresh cilantro leaves and extra jalapeño slices for those who love an extra kick.

Spicy Chicken Cacciatore is a flavor explosion for those who enjoy the bold and fiery side of cuisine. Whether you prefer a mild kick or a scorching heat, you can customize the spice level to your liking.

Chapter 14: Chicken Cacciatore Sides and Accompaniments

Complementing Your Meal with Side Dishes

In this chapter, we'll explore a variety of side dishes and accompaniments that pair perfectly with Chicken Cacciatore. Whether you're looking for bread, pasta, or vegetable pairings, we have a selection of options to enhance your dining experience.

Bread Pairings:

Garlic Bread:

A classic choice, garlic bread is simple to prepare and ideal for soaking up the flavorful sauce of Chicken Cacciatore. Toast slices of French or Italian bread and spread with garlic butter.

Cheesy Breadsticks:

Add an extra layer of indulgence by serving cheesy breadsticks alongside your Chicken Cacciatore. Sprinkle them with Parmesan or mozzarella cheese and serve with marinara sauce for dipping.

Gluten-Free Bread:

For those with gluten sensitivities, consider serving gluten-free bread or rolls. Many gluten-free options are available in stores and can be toasted to perfection.

Pasta Pairings:

Spaghetti:

A classic pasta choice, spaghetti pairs beautifully with Chicken Cacciatore. Toss it with a bit of olive oil, fresh herbs, and grated Parmesan cheese before serving.

Penne:

Penne pasta's tubular shape makes it perfect for capturing the rich sauce of Chicken Cacciatore. Top with fresh basil and a sprinkle of red pepper flakes for added flair.

Gluten-Free Pasta:

If you're following a gluten-free diet, there are numerous gluten-free pasta options available, including rice pasta and corn pasta, that work well with Chicken Cacciatore.

Vegetable Pairings:

Roasted Vegetables:

Roasted vegetables like bell peppers, zucchini, and eggplant complement the flavors of Chicken Cacciatore. Season with olive oil, salt, pepper, and Italian herbs before roasting.

Sautéed Spinach:

A quick and nutritious side, sautéed spinach with garlic and a squeeze of fresh lemon juice adds a vibrant and fresh element to your meal.

Polenta:

Creamy polenta serves as a delightful base for Chicken Cacciatore. Top it with grated Parmesan cheese and fresh herbs for an extra layer of flavor.

Salad Pairings:

Caprese Salad:

The classic Caprese salad featuring ripe tomatoes, fresh mozzarella cheese, and basil drizzled with balsamic glaze is a refreshing and light side dish.

Mixed Greens Salad:

A simple mixed greens salad with a lemon vinaigrette dressing adds a crisp and refreshing contrast to the rich flavors of Chicken Cacciatore.

Caesar Salad:

Caesar salad with homemade croutons and Caesar dressing offers a savory and satisfying accompaniment to your meal.

Dessert Pairings:

Tiramisu:

Conclude your Italian-inspired meal with a classic Tiramisu. This coffee-infused dessert is a delightful way to end the evening.

Cannoli:

Enjoy the sweet and creamy filling of cannoli, a beloved Italian pastry, as a dessert option after your Chicken Cacciatore feast.

With these bread, pasta, vegetable, salad, wine, and dessert pairings, you can create a well-rounded and memorable dining experience to accompany your Chicken Cacciatore. Mix and match these options to suit your preferences and impress your guests.

Chapter 15: Cacciatore-Inspired Sauces and Condiments

Homemade Sauces and Toppings

In this chapter, we'll explore a selection of homemade sauces and condiments inspired by the flavors of Chicken Cacciatore. These versatile additions will elevate your chicken cacciatore experience, allowing you to customize and enhance the dish to your liking.

Cacciatore Marinara Sauce:

Ingredients:

- 1 can (28 ounces) crushed tomatoes
- 1/2 cup red wine (optional)
- 2 cloves garlic, minced
- 1 teaspoon dried oregano
- 1 teaspoon dried thyme
- 1/2 teaspoon red pepper flakes (adjust to taste)
- Salt and pepper to taste

Instructions:

1. In a saucepan, combine crushed tomatoes, red wine (if using), minced garlic, dried oregano, dried thyme, and red pepper flakes.
2. Simmer the sauce over low heat for about 15-20 minutes, stirring occasionally, until it thickens and the flavors meld together.
3. Season with salt and pepper to taste.
4. This marinara sauce is perfect for ladling over your Chicken Cacciatore or using as a dipping sauce for bread.

Olive Tapenade:

Ingredients:

- 1 cup pitted Kalamata olives
- 2 cloves garlic, minced
- 2 tablespoons capers
- 2 tablespoons fresh parsley, chopped
- 2 tablespoons lemon juice
- 2 tablespoons extra virgin olive oil
- Freshly ground black pepper to taste

Instructions:

1. In a food processor, combine pitted Kalamata olives, minced garlic, capers, chopped fresh parsley, and lemon juice.
2. Pulse the mixture until it reaches your desired consistency—some prefer it coarse, while others prefer it smoother.
3. Transfer the olive tapenade to a bowl and stir in extra virgin olive oil.
4. Season with freshly ground black pepper to taste.
5. This flavorful olive tapenade is an excellent condiment to serve alongside your Chicken Cacciatore, adding a burst of briny and zesty flavors.

Roasted Red Pepper Pesto
Ingredients:

- 2 large red bell peppers, roasted, peeled, and seeded
- 1/2 cup fresh basil leaves
- 1/4 cup grated Parmesan cheese
- 1/4 cup pine nuts, toasted
- 2 cloves garlic, minced
- 1/4 cup extra virgin olive oil
- Salt and freshly ground black pepper to taste

Instructions:

1. In a food processor, combine roasted and peeled red bell peppers, fresh basil leaves, grated Parmesan cheese, toasted pine nuts, and minced garlic.
2. Pulse the mixture until it becomes a coarse paste.
3. With the food processor running, slowly drizzle in extra virgin olive oil until the pesto reaches your desired consistency.
4. Season with salt and freshly ground black pepper to taste.
5. This roasted red pepper pesto adds a vibrant and slightly sweet dimension to your Chicken Cacciatore.

These homemade sauces and condiments are versatile and can be used to enhance your Chicken Cacciatore or as accompaniments for bread, pasta, and other dishes. They bring fresh, bold flavors to the table and allow you to customize your dining experience.

Chapter 16: Leftover Makeovers

Creative Ways to Repurpose Leftover Cacciatore

In this chapter, we'll explore inventive ways to give new life to your leftover Chicken Cacciatore, reducing food waste and transforming it into delicious meals that are just as satisfying as the original dish. Get ready to reinvent your leftovers!

Cacciatore-Stuffed Bell Peppers:

Ingredients:

- Leftover Chicken Cacciatore
- 4 large bell peppers, any color
- 1 cup cooked rice or quinoa (optional)
- Shredded mozzarella cheese (optional)

Instructions:

1. Preheat your oven to 375°F (190°C).
2. Cut the tops off the bell peppers and remove the seeds and membranes.
3. Fill each bell pepper with leftover Chicken Cacciatore. If desired, mix in cooked rice or quinoa for added texture and volume.
4. Place the stuffed peppers in a baking dish, cover with aluminum foil, and bake for about 30 minutes.
5. If you like, remove the foil, top each pepper with shredded mozzarella cheese, and bake for an additional 10 minutes until the cheese is bubbly and golden.
6. Serve the Cacciatore-Stuffed Bell Peppers hot, garnished with fresh basil leaves.

Cacciatore Pizza:

Ingredients:

- Leftover Chicken Cacciatore
- Pizza dough (homemade or store-bought)
- Tomato sauce
- Shredded mozzarella cheese
- Sliced bell peppers, olives, or other favorite pizza toppings

Instructions:

1. Preheat your oven to the highest temperature recommended for your pizza dough (usually around 475°F or 245°C).
2. Roll out the pizza dough on a floured surface to your desired thickness.
3. Spread a layer of tomato sauce over the dough.
4. Distribute leftover Chicken Cacciatore evenly over the sauce.
5. Sprinkle shredded mozzarella cheese over the top and add your preferred pizza toppings.
6. Transfer the pizza to a preheated pizza stone or baking sheet and bake for 10-15 minutes or until the crust is golden and the cheese is bubbly.
7. Slice and serve your homemade Cacciatore Pizza.

Cacciatore Quesadillas:
Ingredients:

- Leftover Chicken Cacciatore
- Flour tortillas
- Shredded cheddar cheese
- Sliced bell peppers or onions (optional)

Instructions:

1. Heat a non-stick skillet over medium heat.

2. Place a flour tortilla in the skillet and sprinkle shredded cheddar cheese on one half.
3. Spoon leftover Chicken Cacciatore onto the cheese.
4. If desired, add sliced bell peppers or onions for extra flavor.
5. Fold the tortilla in half to cover the filling, creating a quesadilla.
6. Cook until the tortilla is golden and the cheese is melted, flipping it once.
7. Slice the Cacciatore Quesadilla into wedges and serve with sour cream and salsa.

These creative leftover makeovers breathe new life into your Chicken Cacciatore, ensuring that no delicious bite goes to waste. Whether you're in the mood for stuffed bell peppers, pizza, or quesadillas, you can transform your leftovers into exciting and satisfying dishes.

Chapter 17: Chicken Cacciatore Desserts

Sweet Treats with a Cacciatore Twist

In this chapter, we'll explore desserts that incorporate the flavors and ingredients of Chicken Cacciatore, creating a delightful culinary connection between your main course and dessert. These sweet treats are the perfect way to conclude your Chicken Cacciatore meal.

Cacciatore-Inspired Tiramisu:

Ingredients:

- 1 cup strong brewed coffee, cooled
- 3 tablespoons coffee liqueur (e.g., Kahlúa)
- 3 egg yolks
- 1/2 cup granulated sugar
- 1 cup mascarpone cheese
- 1 teaspoon vanilla extract
- 1 cup heavy whipping cream
- 24 to 30 ladyfinger cookies
- Cocoa powder for dusting
- Dark chocolate shavings for garnish

Instructions:

1. In a shallow dish, combine the cooled brewed coffee and coffee liqueur.
2. In a heatproof bowl, whisk together the egg yolks and granulated sugar. Place the bowl over a pot of simmering water (double boiler) and whisk constantly until the mixture becomes thick and pale, about 5-7 minutes. Remove from heat and let it cool.
3. In a separate bowl, beat the mascarpone cheese and vanilla extract until smooth.

4. In another bowl, whip the heavy whipping cream until stiff peaks form.
5. Gently fold the mascarpone mixture into the egg yolk mixture until well combined.
6. Carefully fold in the whipped cream, creating a light and airy mascarpone mixture.
7. Quickly dip each ladyfinger into the coffee mixture (do not soak) and arrange a layer of dipped ladyfingers in a serving dish.
8. Spread half of the mascarpone mixture over the ladyfingers.
9. Add another layer of dipped ladyfingers and top with the remaining mascarpone mixture.
10. Refrigerate the Cacciatore-Inspired Tiramisu for at least 4 hours or overnight to allow the flavors to meld.
11. Before serving, dust the top with cocoa powder and garnish with dark chocolate shavings.

Cacciatore-Inspired Chocolate Mole:
Ingredients:

- ounces dark chocolate (70% cocoa or higher), chopped

- 1/4 cup almonds, toasted
- 2 dried ancho chilies, soaked, stemmed, and seeded
- 2 cloves garlic, minced
- 1/4 teaspoon ground cumin
- 1/4 teaspoon ground cinnamon
- 1/4 teaspoon ground coriander
- 1/4 teaspoon ground cloves
- 1/4 teaspoon ground allspice
- 1/4 teaspoon salt
- 1/4 cup chicken broth
- 1/4 cup granulated sugar (adjust to taste)
- Vanilla ice cream for serving

Instructions:

1. In a blender or food processor, combine the chopped dark chocolate, toasted almonds, soaked ancho chilies, minced garlic, ground cumin, ground cinnamon, ground coriander, ground cloves, ground allspice, and salt.
2. Blend until the mixture becomes a smooth paste, adding chicken broth as needed to achieve the desired consistency.
3. Transfer the chocolate mole sauce to a saucepan and heat over low heat.
4. Stir in granulated sugar to taste, adjusting the sweetness according to your preference. Simmer for a few minutes to meld the flavors.
5. Serve the Cacciatore-Inspired Chocolate Mole warm over vanilla ice cream.

These Cacciatore-inspired desserts offer a sweet and satisfying conclusion to your Chicken Cacciatore meal. Whether you prefer the classic elegance of Tiramisu or the rich complexity of Chocolate Mole, these treats are sure to delight your taste buds.

Dessert and Wine Pairings:

- For the Tiramisu, consider pairing it with a sweet Italian dessert wine like Vin Santo or a Moscato d'Asti.

- The Chocolate Mole dessert pairs beautifully with a robust red wine such as Cabernet Sauvignon or a dessert wine like Port.

Chapter 18: Tips and Tricks for Perfect Chicken Cacciatore

Troubleshooting Common Issues

In this chapter, we'll provide expert advice and share valuable tips and tricks to help you achieve culinary excellence when preparing Chicken Cacciatore. Whether you're a seasoned chef or a beginner, these insights will ensure your dish turns out perfectly every time.

Chicken Cacciatore Troubleshooting:

1. Overcooked Chicken:

Issue: If your chicken turns out dry and overcooked, it may be because it was simmered for too long.

Solution: Adjust your cooking time. Chicken should be cooked until it reaches an internal temperature of 165°F (74°C). Start checking for doneness around the 15-20 minute mark after adding the chicken to the sauce.

2. Watery Sauce:

Issue: A watery sauce can result from using canned tomatoes with excessive liquid or not allowing the sauce to simmer and reduce.

Solution: Choose canned tomatoes with less liquid, or strain excess liquid from the tomatoes before adding them to the sauce. Simmer the sauce uncovered to allow it to thicken.

3. Lack of Flavor:

Issue: If your Chicken Cacciatore lacks depth of flavor, it may be due to insufficient seasoning or underdeveloped sauce.

Solution: Ensure you season the chicken adequately with salt and pepper before searing. Also, allow the sauce to simmer for a sufficient amount of time to allow the flavors to meld. Taste and adjust the seasoning as needed.

4. Tough Chicken:

Issue: Tough chicken can result from using chicken pieces with bones and skin that haven't been properly browned.

Solution: For tender chicken, use boneless, skinless chicken pieces. If using bone-in, make sure to sear them well on all sides before simmering in the sauce.

5. Sauce Separation:

Issue: Sometimes, the sauce can separate or become oily if the temperature is too high during cooking.

Solution: Maintain a gentle simmer rather than a rolling boil, and avoid overheating the sauce. Stirring the sauce too vigorously can also cause separation, so stir gently when needed.

Expert Advice for Perfect Chicken Cacciatore:

1. Quality Ingredients:

Use high-quality ingredients, including fresh herbs, good-quality canned tomatoes, and wine that you would enjoy drinking. Quality ingredients can significantly enhance the flavor of your dish.

2. Preheat Your Pan:

Ensure your skillet or Dutch oven is properly preheated before searing the chicken. A hot pan helps achieve a beautiful sear on the chicken pieces.

3. Layering Flavors:

Layering flavors is key to a rich and complex sauce. Sauteeing onions, garlic, and peppers first creates a flavorful base. Adding wine, tomatoes, and herbs builds depth.

4. Taste and Adjust:

Taste your sauce throughout the cooking process and adjust the seasonings as needed. Adding a pinch of salt or a dash of wine can make a significant difference.

5. Resting Time:

Allow your Chicken Cacciatore to rest for a few minutes before serving. This allows the flavors to meld, and the sauce will thicken slightly upon resting.

6. Serve with Passion:

When serving, do so with passion and love for the dish. Garnish with fresh herbs, a drizzle of olive oil, or a sprinkle of Parmesan cheese to add that final touch.

By following these tips and tricks and troubleshooting common issues, you'll master the art of preparing perfect Chicken Cacciatore. Remember that practice makes perfect, so don't be discouraged by minor setbacks. With time and experience, your culinary skills will shine.

Chapter 19: Conclusion and Beyond

Summing Up Your Cacciatore Journey

Congratulations! You've embarked on a flavorful journey through the world of Chicken Cacciatore, exploring its classic roots, creative variations, and delightful accompaniments. You've cooked, tasted, and savored the rich flavors and aromas of this beloved Italian dish. As you reach the end of this cookbook, let's summarize your Cacciatore adventure and provide resources for further culinary exploration.

Reflecting on Your Cacciatore Journey:

- You began your journey with the classic Traditional Italian Chicken Cacciatore, mastering the authentic flavors and techniques that have made it a cherished dish for generations.

- You ventured into creative territory with Rustic Vegetable Cacciatore, discovering how to make a vegetarian twist on the Italian classic.

- You added excitement to your culinary repertoire with Chicken Cacciatore with a Twist, exploring innovative fusion recipes and international flavors.

- For those seeking convenience, you learned how to make Slow Cooker and Instant Pot Chicken Cacciatore, saving time without compromising on taste.

- In the quest for healthier options, you discovered Healthy Chicken Cacciatore, savoring lighter versions with reduced fat and calories.

- On busy days, you turned to the simplicity of One-Pot Chicken

Cacciatore, making delicious meals with easy cleanup.

- When outdoor cooking beckoned, you grilled up Grilled Chicken Cacciatore, mastering marinades and grilling techniques.

- For entertaining guests, you dazzled with Chicken Cacciatore for Entertaining, impressing with elegant variations and presentation tips.

- You expanded your culinary horizons with International Cacciatore Flavors, exploring global interpretations of the dish from different cultures.

- To cater to the family, you created Chicken Cacciatore for Kids, serving family-friendly versions and encouraging children to get involved in cooking.

- For those with dietary restrictions, you crafted Gluten-Free Chicken Cacciatore, offering safe and delicious options for gluten-sensitive individuals.

- You ventured into the world of spice with Spicy Chicken Cacciatore, adding a kick with pepper and spice variations.

- You rounded out your meal with Chicken Cacciatore Sides and Accompaniments, mastering bread, pasta, vegetable, salad, wine, and dessert pairings.

- You dabbled in homemade sauces and condiments with Cacciatore-Inspired Sauces and Condiments, enhancing your dishes with personalized flavors.

- To reduce food waste, you explored Leftover Makeovers, creatively repurposing Chicken Cacciatore into new and exciting meals.

- You concluded your culinary exploration with Chicken Cacciatore Desserts, enjoying sweet treats with a Cacciatore twist and dessert and wine pairings.

- Finally, you gained expertise with Tips and Tricks for Perfect Chicken Cacciatore, troubleshooting common issues and honing your skills.

Resources for Further Culinary Exploration:

As you conclude your Chicken Cacciatore journey, here are some resources to further expand your culinary knowledge:

- Cooking Classes: Consider enrolling in cooking classes to learn new techniques, cuisines, and dishes from professional chefs.

- Cooking Websites and Blogs: Explore a multitude of cooking websites and food blogs for endless recipe inspiration, tips, and tricks.

- Cookbooks: Expand your cookbook collection with titles that cater to your culinary interests, whether it's Italian cuisine, global flavors, or healthy cooking.

- Local Food Events: Attend food festivals, farmers' markets, and local food events to sample diverse dishes and ingredients.

- Culinary Workshops: Seek out culinary workshops and seminars in your area to gain hands-on experience and knowledge.

- Food Communities: Join online food communities, forums, and social media groups to connect with fellow food enthusiasts and share ideas.

- Ingredient Exploration: Dive into the world of specific ingredients, such as herbs, spices, or grains, to master their uses and flavors.

Your journey in the kitchen is far from over. Cooking is a lifelong adventure, and there are countless flavors, techniques, and cuisines waiting for you to explore. Remember that the joy of cooking lies in creativity, experimentation, and the shared experience of savoring delicious meals with loved ones.

Thank you for joining us on this Chicken Cacciatore journey. May your kitchen always be filled with the delightful aromas of culinary exploration.

Bon appétit!